EXPLORE OUTER SPACE

QUASARS

by Ruth Owen

WINDMILL
BOOKS

New York

Published in 2013 by Windmill Books, An Imprint of Rosen Publishing
29 East 21st Street, New York, NY 10010

Produced for Windmill by Ruby Tuesday Books Ltd
Editor for Ruby Tuesday Books Ltd: Mark J. Sachner
US Editor: Sara Antill
Designer: Emma Randall
Consultant: Kevin Yates, Fellow of the Royal Astronomical Society

Photo Credits:
Cover, 6–7 © Science Photo Library; 1, 24–25, 26–27, 28–29 © European Southern Observatory; 4–5, 10–11, 12–13, 16–17, 18–19, 20–21 © Shutterstock; 8 © NASA; 9 © NASA, ESA, and The Hubble Heritage Team STScI/AURA; 14–15 © Mike Peel, Jodrell Bank Centre for Astrophysics, University of Manchester; 21 (top left) © NASA and J. Bahcall (IAS); 21 (top right) © NASA, A. Martel (JHU), H. Ford (JHU), M. Clampin (STScI), G. Hartig (STScI), G. Illingworth (UCO/Lick Observatory), the ACS Science Team and ESA; 22–23 © Hubblesite; 23 (top right) © NASA, ESA, and G. Canalizo (University of California, Riverside); 24 (bottom) © ESO/UKIDSS/SDSS.

Library of Congress Cataloging-in-Publication Data

Owen, Ruth, 1967–
  Quasars / by Ruth Owen.
      p. cm. — (Explore outer space)
  Includes index.
  ISBN 978-1-4488-8076-8 (library binding) — ISBN 978-1-61533-605-0 (pbk.) —
  ISBN 978-1-4488-8123-9 (6-pack)
  1. Quasars—Juvenile literature. I. Title.
  QB860.O94 2013
  523.1'15—dc23

                                        2012006733

Manufactured in the United States of America

CPSIA Compliance Information: Batch # B3S12WM: For Further Information contact Windmill Books, New York, New York at 1-866-478-0556

CONTENTS

Extremely Bright and Very Far Away!.................. 4

The Beginning of Time.......................... 6

The Universe Shapes Up 8

Black Holes 10

Quasar Basics 12

Quasi-Stellar Radio Sources.................... 14

Redshift..................................... 16

Measuring in Light Years...................... 18

Looking Back in Time 20

The Births of Quasars......................... 22

The Brightest Object Ever Found................ 24

Back to the Beginning 26

So Much to Learn!............................ 28

Glossary 30

Websites 31

Read More, Index 32

EXTREMELY BRIGHT AND VERY FAR AWAY!

Astronomers have studied **planets, stars,** and faraway **galaxies** for hundreds of years. Then, in the 1960s, astronomers saw something new and very, very bright in space. It wasn't new to the **universe**. It had been there for billions of years. It was something new to **astronomy**, though. We call this object a **quasar!**

So what exactly is a quasar?

A quasar is an extremely bright concentration of energy found at the center of a galaxy. Quasars are fascinating because they are not only super bright, they are also unimaginably far away from us. What's more, quasars are allowing astronomers to see back to the beginnings of time!

The subject of quasars can be mind-boggling, so let's take it step-by-step and start at the very beginning.

That's Out of This World!

The first quasar to be identified was given the name 3C 273. It was trillions and trillions of miles (km) from Earth, and yet it could still be seen with the type of **optical telescope** used by hobby astronomers. This meant that 3C 273 had to be fantastically bright. In fact, it was about two trillion times brighter than our Sun!

Artwork showing a quasar

So when we say the beginning of time, what exactly do we mean? About 13.7 billion years ago, there was nothing. No Earth, no **solar system**, no stars, no universe, no time. Nothing. Then the universe was born!

In one trillion-trillion-trillionth of a second, a tiny, light-filled speck, thousands of times smaller than a pinhead, began to expand. In that fraction of a second, everything that was needed to build the entire universe came into being.

The burning hot fireball of a new universe grew and expanded. In less than a minute, it was billions of miles (km) across and still growing. The universe continued to expand and is still expanding today. This theory of how the universe began is called the big bang theory.

As the universe grew, it began to cool down. Energy turned into matter, and within a few hundred thousand years, the universe was filled with clouds of hydrogen and helium gas. The ingredients for making stars, galaxies, quasars, and everything that we know of were in place.

The big bang

300,000 years later

That's Out of This World!

It's hard to get your head around, but before our universe came into being, there was nothing. You might imagine this nothing as a big, black empty space. But there wasn't even a big black empty space. Just mind-boggling nothing!

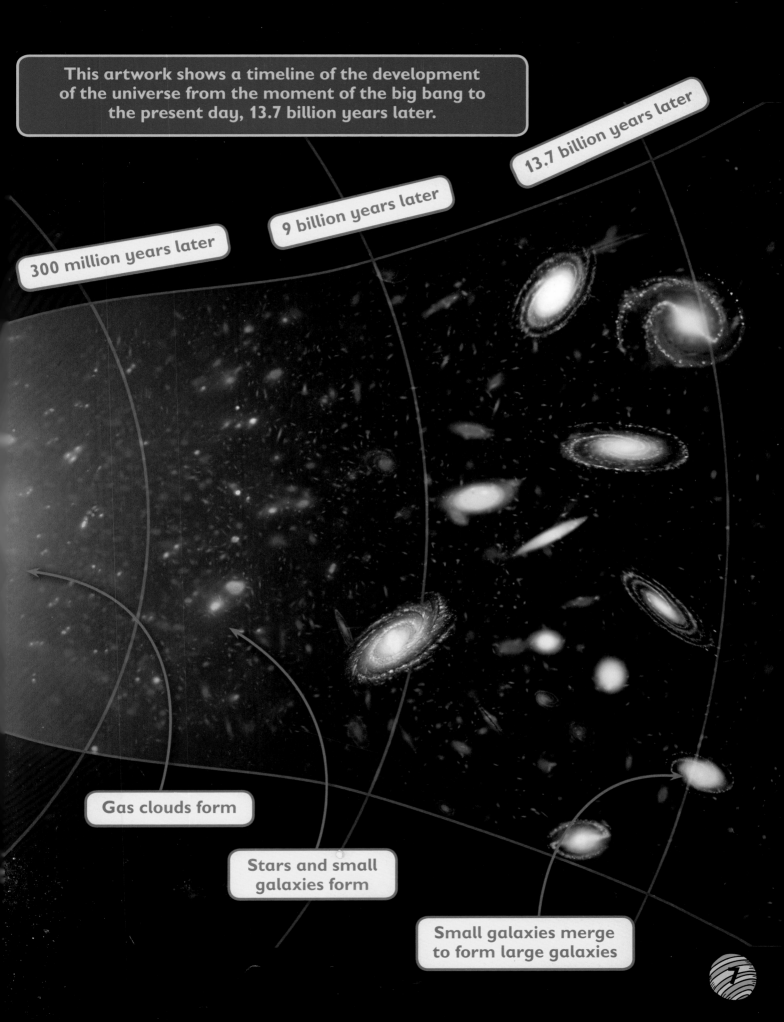

THE UNIVERSE SHAPES UP

Within its first billion years, which isn't such a long time for something that's 13.7 billion years old, the universe became home to such wonders as stars, galaxies, **black holes,** and quasars.

Inside the clouds of gas that had filled the early universe, stars were born. As the gas clouds began to shrink under their own **gravity**, they broke into clumps. The shrinking clumps of gas got hotter and hotter. They became so hot and dense that they ignited and became stars—massive, burning balls of gas!

Huge collections of stars, gas, and dust came together to form galaxies. Many galaxies are shaped like giant disks of stars swirling around a center point. Scientists believe that at the center of just about every galaxy there is a black hole, and at the center of some galaxies, quasars formed.

Arms of stars

This spiral galaxy, named NGC 4414, has a circular shape with arms of stars branching out from the center.

Galaxy center

Bar

Galaxy center

Arm of stars

That's Out of This World!

Our solar system is part of a galaxy called the Milky Way. Our star, the Sun, is just one of up to 400 billion stars that make up this galaxy. Scientists estimate that the Milky Way is around 13.2 billion years old. It formed in the early days of the universe.

BLACK HOLES

Scientists still have a huge amount to learn about quasars, but one thing they do know is that at the heart of every quasar is a supermassive black hole.

A black hole is an incredibly compact, dense object. Its gravitational force is so powerful that nothing that comes close to a black hole can escape being sucked in.

The speed that something must reach to escape another object's gravity is called escape velocity. For example, the Earth's escape velocity is 7 miles per second (11 km/s). That's how fast a rocket must travel to get from Earth into space.

Now, the fastest thing we know of is light. It travels at 186,500 miles per second (300,000 km/s). The gravity of a black hole, however, is so great that its escape velocity is faster than the speed of light. If light, the fastest thing in the universe, cannot escape a black hole, nothing can!

That's Out of This World!

When astronomers look at the places where black holes are, there's nothing to see. Because no light can escape from them, black holes are invisible. We know they are there because of the way they suck in the matter around them!

This artwork shows stars and other matter being pulled toward and into a black hole.

Stars, gas, and dust

Black hole

A swirling disk of matter being pulled into the black hole

QUASAR BASICS

With much still to learn about quasars, here are some things that we do know about these superbright space objects.

Quasars are extremely bright, energetic objects found at the heart of some galaxies. A typical quasar can produce ten trillion times the energy of our Sun. Astronomers use all kinds of telescopes to study quasars, including optical, **X-ray**, and **radio telescopes**.

At the center of a quasar there is a supermassive black hole. The huge and powerful black hole draws in gas, stars, and other matter. As all this matter swirls toward the black hole, it becomes heated. This produces the quasar's energy and incredibly bright light.

Giant jets of material and energy are seen shooting out of the top and bottom of some quasars. These jets can be trillions of miles (km) long!

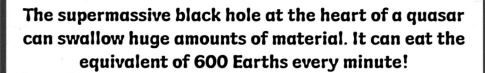

That's Out of This World!

The supermassive black hole at the heart of a quasar can swallow huge amounts of material. It can eat the equivalent of 600 Earths every minute!

Artwork showing a quasar

Jet

Galaxy of stars, gas, and dust

Quasar at center of galaxy

QUASI-STELLAR RADIO SOURCES

The word quasar certainly has an exciting, science fiction-like sound to it. It's short for quasi-stellar radio sources—the original name for quasars.

"Quasi-stellar" means "looking like a star." The "radio sources" part of the name came about because the first quasars were discovered when radio telescopes picked up radio waves emitted by the quasars. A radio telescope doesn't show us an object visually, in the way that an optical telescope does. Radio telescopes pick up radio waves sent out from an object in space.

In the 1950s, astronomers using radio telescopes picked up radio waves coming from very distant objects. Using optical telescopes, they searched space to try to see what was making these radio waves. In 1960, they found quasar 3C 273. They matched up a series of radio waves with light from a very distant starlike object. They were then able to see and identify their first quasar.

That's Out of This World!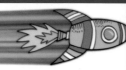

The name "quasi-stellar radio source" was first shortened to "quasar" in 1964 by Chinese-born US scientist Dr. Hong-Yee Chiu. Today, the name quasi-stellar radio source does not accurately describe quasars because many have now been discovered that are very quiet when observed with radio telescopes.

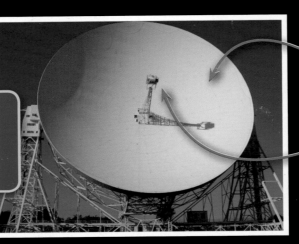

The Lovell Telescope at Jodrell Bank Observatory, in England, is a radio telescope. It was involved in the discovery of many quasars in the 1960s

Dish

Receiver

The telescope's dish collects radio waves and directs them to the telescope's receiver.

REDSHIFT

Scientists figured out that quasars are an extremely long way from Earth by using light.

Ordinary light contains different colors. Scientific instruments can spread light into a spectrum, or rainbow, of the colors red, orange, yellow, green, blue, indigo, and violet.

As an object moves away from Earth, its light shifts toward the red end of the spectrum, and the object appears redder. This is known as **redshift**. The faster an object is moving away from us, the redder its light appears.

Our universe is still expanding and the rate of expansion is speeding up. Distant objects in space, such as quasars, are moving away from us more quickly than closer objects. They therefore have a great redshift. When scientists first saw quasars, the red light coming from these objects told them that quasars are extremely distant!

The background of these pages shows the color spectrum of light. The colors are violet, indigo, blue, green, yellow, orange, and red.

Stars

A distant quasar

A distant quasar has great redshift and looks like a tiny red dot.

That's Out of This World!

Today, astronomers have discovered and identified more than 200,000 quasars.

MEASURING IN LIGHT YEARS

When it comes to measuring the distance from Earth to a quasar, miles (km) are just not big enough to do the job.

To measure enormous distances in space, astronomers use a unit of measurement called a **light year**. As we saw earlier, light is the fastest thing in the universe, and it travels at about 186,500 miles per second (300,000 km/s). Therefore, in a year, light can travel 5.8 trillion miles (9.4 trillion km).

So, something in space that is one light year from Earth is 5.8 trillion miles (9.4 trillion km) away. That is certainly a huge distance, but it seems like nothing in the vastness of space!

The first quasar to be identified, 3C 273, is 2.4 billion light years from Earth!

That's Out of This World!

If an astronomer had to use miles to measure and record how far away quasar 3C 273 is from Earth, the measurement would look like this: 14,000,000,000,000,000,000,000 miles (22,500,000,000,000,000,000,000 km). That's not very practical for reading or writing!

Light traveling
through space

LOOKING BACK IN TIME

Today, we know that quasar 3C 273 is a bright, powerful object, powered by a black hole, in the center of a galaxy.

We also know that it is 2.4 billion light years away from Earth. That's amazing, but not just because it's a huge distance. It's amazing because it means that the light we see coming from 3C 273 has been traveling through space for 2.4 billion years.

What astronomers see when they look at 3C 273 is not how the quasar looks today, but how it looked 2.4 billion years ago. If we wanted to know what this quasar is doing today, we'd have to wait 2.4 billion years for its current light to reach us!

This is why quasars are so interesting to astronomers. They allow us to look back in time to see what was happening in our universe billions of years ago.

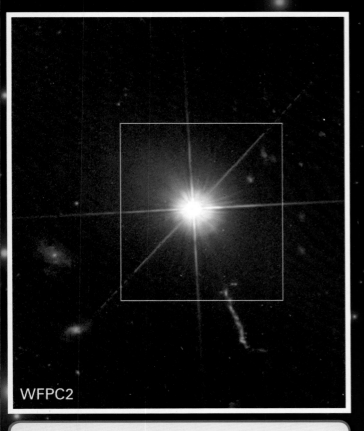

WFPC2

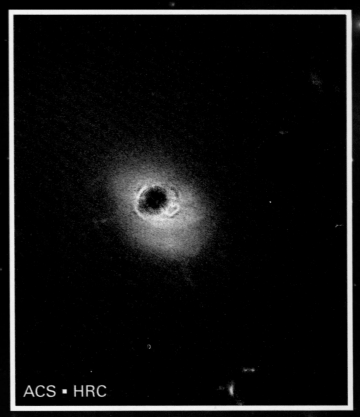

ACS · HRC

Quasar 3C 273 photographed by Hubble's Wide Field Planetary Camera 2

Quasar 3C 273's host galaxy revealed in an image by Hubble's Advanced Camera for Surveys (ACS)

That's Out of This World!

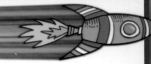

Using two different cameras on the Hubble Space Telescope, it's possible to see different views of quasar 3C 273. The Wide Field Planetary Camera 2 image (left) shows the incredibly bright light of the quasar. When Hubble's Advanced Camera for Surveys (ACS) is used (right), it's possible to block out the quasar's light to reveal its home galaxy. Studying the quasar's galaxy and black hole may help astronomers understand more about how quasars are formed and how they act.

THE BIRTHS OF QUASARS

In 2007, images from the Hubble Space Telescope revealed some very interesting information about a quasar named MC2 1635+119.

The Hubble image showed arcs, or shells, of stars traveling away from the center of the quasar's home galaxy, like ripples in a pond when a stone is tossed into the water. This movement of stars told astronomers that at some point in the galaxy's history, it had collided with another galaxy. The collision caused the movement of stars, but it may also have caused huge quantities of matter to be funneled into the galaxy's black hole. The clashing of the two galaxies may have provided so much fuel to the black hole that it enabled a quasar, powered by the black hole, to form.

This is just one of the theories that astronomers are studying in their quest to understand what makes quasars burst into life.

That's Out of This World!

Images from the Hubble Space Telescope are helping astronomers learn more about quasars. Hubble orbits Earth outside of our **atmosphere**. Unlike telescopes on Earth, Hubble can detect distant objects in space more clearly because the movement of our atmosphere does not blur its view.

Hubble image of MC2 1635+119

Hubble Space Telescope

Earth

23

THE BRIGHTEST OBJECT EVER FOUND

In June 2011, a group of European astronomers discovered a quasar that was brighter than anything previously found in the universe!

The quasar was discovered using the European Southern Observatory's Very Large Telescope (VLT) and other telescopes around the world. The team of astronomers had been carefully searching for quasars in deep space for five years when they made their amazing discovery.

The quasar has been named ULAS J1120+0641. The superbright quasar shines with the light of 63 trillion Suns. It is powered by a supermassive black hole that has a mass two billion times the mass of our Sun.

The newly discovered quasar wasn't just the brightest object ever discovered, though. It was also the most distant quasar ever to be found!

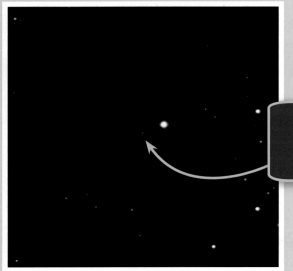

Quasar ULAS J1120+0641 can be seen as a faint red dot in the center of this image.

That's Out of This World!

Scientist Daniel Mortlock, who was part of the team that discovered the new quasar, says of looking for quasars, "It's like sifting for gold (searching for tiny nuggets of gold in water). You're looking for something shiny!"

The four Unit Telescopes that together are called the Very Large Telescope (VLT) at the European Southern Observatory (ESO) in the Atacama Desert, in Chile.

BACK TO THE BEGINNING

When astronomers discovered quasar ULAS J1120+0641, they realized that they were looking back almost to the beginning of time.

The quasar was so far from Earth that its light had taken nearly 13 billion years to reach us! When astronomers looked at their new discovery, they were looking back in time to a moment just 770 million years after the big bang. They were seeing a quasar in action in the very earliest days of our universe.

It's amazing to think that the quasar is now long gone. We would have to wait another 13 billion years to know what is happening in that part of the universe today. For now, however, scientists are getting a valuable look at what was happening in one tiny corner of our universe soon after the universe came into being.

An artist's view of how ULAS J1120+0641 might look.

That's Out of This World!

The light from ULAS J1120+0641 has taken nearly 13 billion light years to reach us. So it should follow that the quasar is 13 billion light years from Earth. It is, however, now over 28 billion light years from Earth. This is because the universe is expanding, and the quasar is moving away from us!

SO MUCH TO LEARN!

Astronomers have only been studying quasars for about 60 years. New information is discovered about these distant objects all the time, and any theory may soon be disproved by new discoveries.

One thing that astronomers are eager to know is how quasars come into being. Do quasars occur when two galaxies collide? Does something as yet unknown happen to a previously quiet and normal galaxy to cause a bright, powerful quasar to form at its center?

Maybe quasars are a phase that young galaxies go through when there is lots of matter to feed the galaxy's black hole and power the quasar. When all the gas and dust have been burned up by the black hole or turned into stars, does the quasar die and the galaxy settle down?

One thing is for sure when it comes to quasars—this area of astronomy still has far more questions than answers!

Around the world, astronomers and telescopes scan the skies looking for quasars and answers to the mysteries that still surround these incredibly bright, distant objects.

That's Out of This World!

Many astronomers believe that our galaxy, the Milky Way, may once have been a quasar. Over billions of years, our home galaxy settled down.

Stars in our home galaxy, the Milky Way

The four telescopes of the European Southern Observatory's Very Large Telescope (VLT)

GLOSSARY

astronomer (uh-STRAH-nuh-mer)
A scientist who specializes in the study of outer space.

astronomy (uh-STRAH-nuh-mee)
The branch of science that studies the universe and all the forces, objects, and matter in outer space.

atmosphere (AT-muh-sfeer)
The layer of gases surrounding a planet, moon, or star.

black hole (BLAK HOHL)
A region of space around a very small and extremely massive object, usually formed by a collapsed star, within which the gravitational field is so strong that not even light can escape.

galaxy (GA-lik-see) A group of stars, gas, dust, and other objects held together in outer space by gravity.

gravity (GRA-vuh-tee) The force that causes objects to be attracted toward Earth's center or toward other physical bodies in space, such as stars or planets.

light year (LYT YIR) The distance light can travel in a year—more than 5.8 trillion miles (9.4 trillion km).

optical telescope
(OP-tih-kul TEH-leh-skohp)
A telescope that uses lenses, mirrors, or both to gather the visible light that is given off by an object in order to create a magnified image of the object.

planet (PLA-net) An object in space that is of a certain size and that orbits, or circles, a star.

quasar (KWAY-zar)
Short for "quasi-stellar radio source"; a distant object in deep space that gives off huge amounts of light and energy. Scientists believe quasars form the center of certain galaxies or represent a stage in the development of galaxies.

radio telescope
(RAY-dee-oh TEH-leh-skohp)
A type of antenna used to detect radio waves or radiation and the sources of those waves.

redshift (RED-shift) A way of detecting the speed and distance of an object based on the fact that the spectrum, or range, of visible light is actually made up of many different colors, and that a source of light that is moving away from us will appear red;

the more red that is detected, the faster the object is moving away, and therefore the farther it is from us.

solar system (SOH-ler SIS-tem) The Sun and everything that orbits around it, including asteroids, meteoroids, comets, and the planets and their moons.

star (STAR) A body in space that produces its own heat and light through the release of nuclear energy created within its core. Earth's Sun is a star.

universe (YOO-nih-vers) All of the matter and energy that exists as a whole, including gravity and all the planets, stars, galaxies, and contents of intergalactic space.

X-rays (EKS-rayz) In astronomy, radiation that is given off by objects in space that produce incredible heat, such as stars and quasars, and that may be detected by instruments on Earth or launched into space.

WEBSITES

For web resources related to the subject of this book, go to: www.windmillbooks.com/weblinks and select this book's title.

READ MORE

Asimov, Isaac, and Richard Hantula. *Black Holes, Pulsars, and Quasars.* Isaac Asimaov's 21st Century Library of the Universe: Near and Far. New York: Gareth Stevens, 2005.

DeCristofano, Carolyn Cinami. *A Black Hole Is Not a Hole.* Watertown, MA: Charlesbridge Publishing, 2012.

Solway, Andrew. *Quantum Leaps and Big Bangs!: A History of Astronomy.* Chicago: Heinemann-Raintree, 2005.

INDEX

A
astronomers, 4, 10, 14, 17–18, 20, 22, 24, 26, 28–29
astronomy, 4, 28
atmosphere, 22

B
big bang, 6–7, 26
black holes, 8, 10–12, 20–22, 24, 28

C
Chiu, Dr. Hong-Yee, 14

E
Earth, 4, 6, 10, 12, 16, 18, 20, 22–23, 26–27
escape velocity, 10
European Southern Observatory (ESO), 24–25, 29

G
galaxies, 4, 6–9, 12–13, 20–22, 28–29
gases, 6–8, 11–13, 28
gravity, 8, 10

H
helium, 6
hydrogen, 6
Hubble Space Telescope, 21–23

J
Jodrell Bank Observatory, 14–15

L
light, 10, 14, 16–18, 20–21, 26–27
light years, 18, 20, 27
Lovell Telescope, 14–15

M
Milky Way, the, 9, 29
Mortlock, Daniel, 25

O
optical telescopes, 4, 12, 14

P
planets, 4

Q
quasi-stellar radio sources, 14

R
radio telescopes, 12, 14–15
radio waves, 14–15
redshift, 16–17

S
solar system, 6, 9
speed of light, 10
spiral galaxies, 8
stars, 4, 6–9, 11–14, 17, 22, 28–29
Sun, 4, 9, 12, 24

T
time, 4, 6, 26

U
universe, 4, 6, 8, 10, 16, 18, 20, 24, 26–27

V
Very Large Telescope, 24–25, 29

X
X-ray telescopes, 12